East of the Sun,
West of the Moon

And what you do not know is the only thing you know
And what you own is what you do not own
And where you are is where you are not.

East Coker, Four Quartets

– T.S. Eliot

To Mamoni

East of the Sun,
West of the Moon

Taz Rahman

Seren is the book imprint of
Poetry Wales Press Ltd.
Suite 6, 4 Derwen Road, Bridgend,
Wales, CF31 1LH

www.serenbooks.com
Follow us on social media @SerenBooks

The right of Taz Rahman to be identified as
the author of this work has been asserted in accordance
with the Copyright, Designs and Patents Act, 1988.

ISBN: 978-1-78172-734-8
ebook: 978-1-78172-735-5

A CIP record for this title is available from the British Library.

The publisher acknowledges the financial assistance of the Books Council of Wales.

Cover painting: Anna Amalia Coviello, 'East of the Sun, West of the Moon'.

Printed in Bembo by 4edge Limited, Essex.

Contents

Yashica 635   7
Seamstress   9
Butter   10
Trap Arachnids for Rainy Days   12
Internal Reliquary   14
Teach Jackdaws Avionics   17
Bread of Heaven   18
A Morning Walk   20
I Want to See Your Face in Every Kind of Light   21
The Free State of Roath   23
Animal Wall   25
A Pond for All Eels   32
Stars siphon narcissus so   33
Learning to Write a Cantabile for Tawny,
    Sooty, Eurasian   34
Muktijoddha   36
Permission   37
Strange Fruit   40
Turning Saints into the Sea   44
The Nearness of You   45
Drama/Trauma   46
East of the Sun, West of the Moon   50
Chocolate   52
Missa Solemnis   54
Amygdala   56
Sanctuary   58
Snapdragons Need the Bulk of Bumblebees to
    Force Open the Flower   60
Anda   62
The Substrate of a Rose   64
Ramadan   66
Aurora Out of Time   68
What Are You Doing the Rest of Your Life   69

Acknowledgements   71

Yashica 635

I pine curves, guavas, sofedas, a wave arching
back falling flat on its face. I want to convince

you that the jackfruit in its afternoon spikes is
an inaudible layer, inedible like the past;

the tongue may crave its dorsal surface to levitate,
the lateral border to swell, but even if the tip

opens to the dollop of ripe, the lingual tonsil shall
rise up, rebel, repel the past. A light is trying to creak

through the floorboards, its somnambulant
gait is feral as the hills, sand dunes, days out

to Savar at the Martyr's Memorial under a katha,
my father winding our faces, shapes, concrete

and miles far and near – not even the eyes could
see how the fingers folded spindles of flies

groaning inside the unbroken peel cage of Langra
aam, my mother's expert fingers hesitant to scrape

off the whole afternoon. I observe catharsis
to heal the unhealable, let cellulose acetate puncture

chemical dips. Once my father walked a whole year
along a sea path filled in the Beirut dust, his feet

flattening the desert and its stylites, and back East,
clicks turned into clinks, brass spoons stirring clouds

of milk in Moulvibazar tea. I want to tell you
about the curtains, handstitched in forgotten shades

unfurling a decade: independence, the rise of a nation,
an assassination, a metallic blue Civic smelling

the same sky as sourdough Sobhanbagh, quieter than
beetles taking refuge in the exterior cornices

of verandas before a storm, and beyond those
curtains, crayon-stained, how my sister learnt

to crawl. But, I am not ready. Let ash stain
the Dhanmondi sky in evenings wearing red after

each storm, turn lilacs into violets – it is possible
to carve patterns, trap lipids,

fan unfettered the indelible to embalm the body
as a spillage of trapped light.

Katha: a hand-stitched light blanket, sometimes intricate embroidered, common in
Bangladesh and East Bengal, India.

Langra Aam: a famous variety of mango very common along the eastern regions of the
Indian subcontinent.

Seamstress

I have taught myself to repair the torn.
Yesterday, I stitched life back
into an Arctic fox – used the leftovers

to patch unruly splits in rusty old slacks –
learning to plug gaps, mend cracks.
Flesh sears fibre, seams fracture,

come apart, buttons hang loose,
mid-winter cracks heels;
once in a while, something

sticks out its tongue, licks the bits
poking through finger-cut-out gloves,
fingers that thumb rain, index undone,

press the hole on a slow drifting boat
into the wind's tail unconcerned of
shore or bottom first. But I can fix it all,

the repairs are impressive, they might
just hold in the rust and arrears. Now,
there is an emerging cross, brown

Narcissus standing tall, proud, in love
with itself, boring the duvet of summers
past. It must be plugged, goddesses

appeased. I must be the alterer,
seamstress, carpenter, find cubs to fur,
new hands to mitten, paper over cracks.

Butter

Sa-re-ga-ma-pa-dha-ni-sa
sang
the curtains.

The sacred hob
slung low,
purring blue

in low stool squats
frothing
shingara, tikia,

splash of soyabean
splattering air;
in the corner,

the mighty kolshi,
sweat brimming
in earthen rings

– my grandmother
called it kolosh
in her back of throat 'h' –

coconut oil in my mother's hair
smearing what I breathed in.
On days she stayed in,

sound of pestle
ground holdi
churning turmeric,

daal bore holes into plates we ate
–thin like my father loved–
floating peyajeebereshta,

burnt onion tadpoles
swimming to the edge of his mouth,
his moustache dipping

into silent lake sips
of water
frozen in the fridge.

My mother took the butter
out of the fridge each morning,
spread our days with it.

Trap Arachnids for Rainy days

Lone droplets stare at brittle cracks

spilling Cathays to Roath. All night

the tracks seep moisture for stars

shredding hesitancy to fool

the epiglottis, let in bulbous heads,

wreath champs. Nights tremble

in puddles, beetles squirm inside

biscuit tins, chide Bhagwan, Ishwar,

Allah. The male is a glove cushioned

to dampen blades, nauseate rust.

Organed on ends of palps, fused

heads leer at thoraxes, the sun

cantaloupes carrot to apricot, a silken

sheet funnel retreats at the back. Slats

dust imprints in herring-bone

for the dead post coitus, lone ants

creed ceilings so cobwebs can swaddle

love, shield a jawline. Eyes become

empty seats at the cinema pining to cup

buttocks. Clouds grind follies in moisture,

splashes become pearls, streams run down

panes, lubricate songs for dead ants.

The fattened chin sits upright ringside

to warm the secrets of cha, a window-seat.

Internal Reliquary

White lines at a crossing
    tongue grit
      whispering incantations
to a low-sprung bed in a room
for bodies refusing to stand
under the shower
    wash off the night air.

I clutch bodies
    let go to reveal
another layer
juice skin
    coddling tendons.

I peel curtains
    rent them
    back to the walls
open a window
    let the sunshine brood walnuts.

A space may contain
    physical forms
the expanse between them

    seconds
multiplied by divisions.

A space may contain
a winter
    when nothing ripens

spring
summer
    a ripening avocado.

I want to preserve the dust
    from a dusk:

when the rose quartz
a membrane
        off the pericardium

dangling from the neck
        is not
        pressed between skins

and the walls
rent back the walnuts
        to regurgitate
Mehldau, McBride, Redman
        blading, twisting, plucking
        dampening a blow.

A dressing gown eases its folds
        not far enough

a belt is pulled tight
        to mow skin

the trance of fibres
        scheming touches

for calibrated time
to cease
        the pesky chords
        winding distant roars

chords
        burning Notre Dame
        London rebelling extinction
a hundred arrested.

And, in Albany Road
        above a chicken shop
in a room too safe

a voice on the radio
     is pickling burdock
to make it taste
     like lotus roots.

I want to hold
     on to the space
     salting stardust.

Teach Jackdaws Avionics

The sun does not fuss, days survive, clematis curates purple
in alleyways for blackbirds to core arcs in hunger, sing

to flowers, discourse evenings stretched on grass. Fingers
frack surfaces, erupt touch, catch aphids, time, molten

cores, questions – questions like why is the asphodel so
hardy in its narrow grass-like leaves, the stem elongating

the handsomest spike in white so unheard lives may
meadow in its six flirting petals. The sun hides in roof-lines

past noon, enters fan vaults warming chimneys to seduce
the fattest pigeon lit like silty grains carrying miles. May

bees shake their own cowbells, vine inquisition into mahonia
blooming too early in inclines no right to smile, a kingdom of

floating purr climbs a wall, wags tail like another species, in
the field nearby goats cough, neigh soft, thud hooves, pretend

to be stallions feeding a chorus of want wanting to stir, morning
chairs touch napes of human arms inside a high street café, pine

flesh, the leftover rose, its wilting stem aching to sit upright, trace
the night gone, one last glance at something to trail lost snails.

Bread of Heaven

The 64 km long river Taff enters Cardiff at Taff's Well flowing south into Cardiff Bay.

Snowdrops writhing / late daffodils peeking before / time a fervent pink
/ peeving through lime-pine-oak-ash-hornbeam /

a March trying / to convince this land / is past wyverns / that some
version of / pink is washed / off blood /

I am a sun-burnt / slap mottling Taff / which monster / threw me in
when / in time present and time past /

a serpent mane / meanders as steam / climbs up a castle keep /
red-white-green nurdling aloft / valley-lake-brae /

spring melanges as green / white is a layer of / terns swallowing a sea /
the end of a / beginning /

morning dew / lifting / chapel hush / chittering gossip / tween the crow
and tigerworm / men-women-undefined / a rush / a glance / a dance /

driftwood stacked / off / February flood / lock in feet / plead / plot /
connive every trick to / make ankles stick /

at noon I am still / a shadow / rat-tat-tat / silhouettes darken to / keep
me contained / what came / before what / to submerge every ridge-
fossil-hollow /

boulders cwtch / compelled to justify presence / cough / let the water /
percolate cracks /

I let the sound stutter / let gurgles purify each bank / wobble each
bridge /

does the quarry these / stones came from miss / the parts hacked /

is there a requiescat trembling / the grieving sitar / mourning this loss in
/ mass /

the sun dips past two / stones have / as much business / with the river /
as I /

neither may / claim / utility /

we mullion a sturdy back / to stand / an inch higher / quench a thirst /
something to give back / a debt to repay /

where home / is / in the shower / I sequester dirt /

debtors hide / in the rings under my chin /

bubbles forage the / naval in search of a / songbird / lather a mist arching
/ my brow /

the let gone line to lick / the mends of / a hernia /

evening / falls / on the afternoon /

a procession retreats to / each corners of / the river like the cleanest
laundered / sheets / pens sheathed / keyboards wiped clean of writs /
perruques drizzled in / ale-prosecco-vino /

I chew / my own skin / tear up / the daily bread in / all its wheaten
spelt / sometimes stale / flatten the pieces for / beaks to grasp / I keep
the olives / to salinate my own cuts /

one day I / shall conjure / a typhoon / I shall colour in / a passant / red
/ gather all the plastic / from storms gone / clattering the banks /

I shall stop / asking / where each carrier / came from /

what the river has / smeared them in / why a pigeon hatched in / the
backyard asks me / to reveal / my palm each dawn /

paint lips in saliva / slaughter all memory / flow / feed / be fed /

A Morning Walk

The dark is still
a wireworm wriggling
in cruds of earth.

Unformed gloom,
jackdaws swooping
as black clouds

above pines,
birdsong shadowing
each leaf

walk – evade nothing
rain, sleet, wind –
wake dawn

hear the grass
still each tip,
each reflection

an imprisonment
in pools of dew,
swallows submerged

in kicks and throws.

I Want to See Your Face in Every Kind of Light

On the surface
of Ely
mouths gasp
for permission.

Up above
dragonflies the size
of a segment of finger
chase dreams

each other
faces collide
curving to mount
yesterday from behind

I want to plunge my face
into something
in the depth of small
nestling over silence

in half-flight
in numberless hours
measured in berries
ripenedto tremble.

I want to honey
with nimble lips
a forest yoga
under a blanket

melting careless helebores
in the dark
an unfinished
infusion in bodies

pressed
to a mindless tangle
of tongues
till the ivies get us.

If I sit
till midnight
watch amoon
pulsatefollicles

we are still
too far.

The Free State of Roath

If you were on my mind
night and day, if I forgot to eat,
sleep, pray,

on its palsied wings
a cormorant disrobed our past
spanning a whole

Taff coralled in versions
of an upstream self, droplets
tremored rocks

on no motive
to engender splash, blame
it on a daisy. The very

thought of you
is thirst, my words weave
a city far off caves,

canaries measure
wild uneven with theodolites,
some days

I force a chord
playing an arpeggio filling
an entire freckle,

warm coves
the insides of an arum,
the largest pure white

spathes an enclosure
fingering the spikes to lily
leaves. My tongue

is seasoned
in spooning arrows for Eucharist,
I floret days

without voices
to shrill my walks, I think
your top lip is

a delirious roller
passing up a storm, incubating
needs, a primer

on primal
surging lockdowns, shrubbing
f-sharp tugged to sweeten

the wettest patches
serving no purpose but widen
nights, leave marks

on a kingfisher warming
another bank on another walk
for a body sulling

snapdragons, deadheading
an ox-eye, a hatless lemon
in the evening blur.

Animal Wall

A whimsical heron, sometimes a songbird, sometimes, in human form dips in and out of tales old and new, around Cardiff Castle; one spring, for the first time, the wandering soul feels a sense of belonging.

I

After the pews are cold
after morning service
after the loiterers are gone
St. John sniffs the city stalls.

Sprat and turbot at market's gate
figs and fennel in autumn mist
waft of Cornwall
Ten Feet Tall.

Evening falls on red-cheeked
Adam, Jamie, Annmarie
who drink dry the skull of Glyndwr
clutching their little red books.

Old Owain under the cover
in a mass brawl
gawks at an oval
eighty thousand growl.

Here, I saw Gareth Edwards
hands in pocket
sniffing cinnamon
walk pass the Christmas stall.

★

Past the American king
under the barrister's chamber
into the arcade
then turn left

fifty steps north
stands the wall
where in a gale
I first met Annabelle.

That night
my brolly protests
in feeble fight, bows
in respect inside out

lost Anna, bell-grey heron
soaring above the Nile
dunking Geneva
steaming Thames

a short haul after
in the dead of night
she screams
on the banks of Taff.

Over a cuppa
astride me
pinned to a bed
she flaps:

of all the castles I've seen
from Bushey to Brecon
never have I seen
an animal wall.

II

Damp seeps through
the fort of Taff
the water drips
the visitor strays

shadows run
day and night
in sentries fossilised
towers eek saints

Teilo, Illtud, Canna
to the low hills west
the castle grouts
growls, curates rot.

North-wall brambles
the magnolia shed
swallows stir, squirrels sew
a pink-white quilt.

Magpies descend,pattern
feast on succulent worms
observe as corvids do
in watchful nods.

★

Priscilla pelican
lost her eyes
eyes that once glinted
morning to coal.

On her wall mutter
the racoon, the beaver
the vulture, the wolf
the lynx shakes head

washes up seal
snorts dry anteater
the heron, daubed in grime
stills the animal wall.

★

Life on walls:
a moat parched
in hot summer thirst
schools break

summer swarms
upon the teenage lithe
bewitched fragrant weed
lined next to twisted dreams

armies of St. John
virgins for St. Mary
baffled monks at
Greyfriars, Blackfriars

grope Molly, Charlie, Mandy
the sky sings late in dark
a hymn to sobriety
in nightjar prayer.

★

By the wall
in pitched bereave
the lonely man
who once was a boy

the night love-spooned
moon-beams now so quiet
pat the coat-tails
of old Captain Morgan.

III

Steps to the north
past the moat
a path held in metal strips
stones crushed

sprinkled on gravel,
to the side
is the foot deep brook.
In tiny steps

the pupper
dips his toes
runs down water
stirs mud.

Wild mushrooms
yellow, pink
sundrenched soaks
doggo splash.

★

Off the steps
the metal strips
the old path that lace
morning trysts

daisies hold back
footsteps
the chancer
pleasure-seeker

man and dog
woman and mog
dandelions look over the side
dance The Royal Welsh −

Bergman
Harold Arlen
Hoagy Carmichael
sings Annabelle

What are you doing the rest of your life
North and South and East and West of your life
I have only one request of your life
That you spend it all with me

her voice soaring
above the bridge
wood croaking
spinning spokes

the path of man
stare down late April
a wild garlic bloom
across the bank.

IV

Under a giant leaf
the last note sung
wakes heron
coos goodbye

in her green-eyed smile
to the mute swans
sweet glide
above the notes of long

over the arched-low-bridge
where the moat stream
hides in ventricles of moss
the castle flares

in a queen
the paths of Bute
gleamsa coot
and lotus stream

there in the shade
of the hunched tree
by the canal unknown
rests Annabelle.

★

Zephyr rides
late in Spring
the mist turns mizzle
murmurs a toad

enraptured flies cling heron
there in the canal green
springs new life
to sit upon the castle wall

A Pond for All Eels

How vibernum clatters primrose
    the heron greys spring
        hangs like a lamp giving off gloom

how the twigs lurch at each crotch
    as bodies float on the wings
        of their macs

how eels electric
    transcutaneously, motor
        neurons

how sparrows embroider decisions
    in brown not saying a word
        braille bushes

I want to make room for the body
    for its speechless want to be
        clattered

I want to pretend that
    a day was a night, blame
        the breeze

some eels emit a weak pulse
    to navigate, find prey, melt icebergs
        linger in a set of eyes

I want to be a stream
    discover the shallows
        where duckweed congeals

green and dark eyes
    bloat spring, hum bells
        kill time.

Stars siphon narcissus so

she can stay in this poem for the day I learn
to contract the tongue, extend to its furthest,
go sideways, strut movements to fit syllables,
ask my sister how she watches our mother
comatose for 30 sols. Seasons come and go,

Venus nears the Pleiades, Mercury in its
sluggish ellipsis – lunar libration favours
eastern limbs like mine – past Saturn, past
Jupiter, past the lyrid meteor of a lurid
Bhagavat consecrating Golgotha, February

marks borders in squares, a fringe of warm,
groundsel swells the crouching grass, scolds
bitterness, willow weeps a severed anterior,
in March she went square, April still far.
Magpies line a lone gaze – it counts 'two

for joy' if I spot two in successive blinks?
Any answer would do. Her last chide
– my last search – cornershop MSG. The
wheelchair spins before the boarding call,
airports are the loneliest goodbyes, *five*

more minutes please, my slashed tongue
for a morsel of gajor. When I say 30th I
mean morning tea stringing a scryer, a gap
under the fire-door to lure draft, Munkar
Nakirchitter, inferno-purgatario-paradiso,
eyes black-black-black-black-black coda.

MSG: monosodium glutamate is a common flavour enhancer in Asian cuisine.

Gajor: carrot in Bengali, the main ingredient for a popular homemade sweet.

Learning to Write a Cantabile
for Tawny, Sooty & Eurasian

Scene: Black Mountain College, Talgarth,
climate change retreat.

Conifers bed an anorexic moon
        for a stream in need, I replace
want with cicadas a season late
        in a mountain that is a hill
by a river that is a brook

for cockatoos who are wood
        pigeons rouging dawn daring
apples part red parting green
        to squeeze themselves fresh
as September thirst. I gather

groans as songs, hoard rain –
        the droplets are doe-eyed
to berry the bite of the elder,
        whisk wasps to illicit corners
of dusk with owls watching

over bodies who know how
        to preserve rocks the way
hymns carry stadiums down
        Taff, caress snapdragons like
it is a mystery, recycle each

fall, turn up with no history,
        no previous to drink storms,
the gust tenting the night
        two pegs short. Goats shrivel
mornings in mist, grass-tops

snare syllabic dew, fatsias
       brood in the first-light
cadenza,
brew sacrificial tea peddling
       cosmos to the denier – time
is a polity – we come, we go,

soothe tigers, breathe soil,
       cement glass, mortar, clear
hilltops, breed, bleed, pluck,
       cover each inch of loam
for bees to whisper never.

Muktijoddha

Incarnate spring, flower daisies, let red rim white,
lips, sunhats, umbrellas to cobble blossom, braid

town-squares, shade the past in light, fountains
to scald flames, tufts of smoke, that unspoken

stench of flesh to nurse the moribund back to life.
Shuffle through the numbers, count creaks in the

futon under the weight of days, let buttons turn
bombs into a concerto, projectiles to quarternotes,

drones to balloons. Some days, I press zero just
to feel, reveal what spring is like in Jupiter and

Mars with all the goats dead, a screenburnt ghost
tatters a gogglebox, gods blink speeches pouring

sympathy, Krishna slays Shishupala, boots trample
milkthistle ordered to press a button, bloodshot

thumbs on triggers, the finger-flesh whitens – splatter
no milk-drops. In the distance, a cornershop bursts

all aisles of froth semi-skinned churning a floor into
an alba of wisteria floribunda pure as baby-cheeks,

heliotropes lay petals to cup a ceiling crumbling in
dignity – rubble can carve a magnificat to beauty. I

secrete canticles to dress bruises, flatten the notes
to clot blood, joba-phul whistles the sins of kittens.

Muktijoddha: freedom fighter, the young who took up arms during the war of liberation in Bangladesh. The survivors bore emotional scars throughout their lives wherever they lived. The 1971 war between India and Pakistan, which resulted in the creation of independent Bangladesh, was a direct result of unresolved partition related issues from 1947.

Joba-phul: A blood-red hibiscus common in the eastern regions of the Indian subcontinent.

Permission

An unfinished tulip
in every hole

indecision   inaction   emaciation

what would
our fathers say?

a diaphanous groan smearing sebum

Fathers
who held up
swords   quills   artillery

Polashi   Seringapatam   Dehli   Faridpur   Dhaka

struck treaties with Napoleon
deceived by Wellesley to live like a lion

for   the   whole   five   minutes?

I am
a tableful
of cake crumbs

Victoria Sponge   Battenberg   Dundee   Madeira   BhapaPitha

a rocky road of brownies secreting caramel

sometimes, a swole river salted to taste

a fresh green scent
a floral *Parfum Du Jour*
no longer bottled

I am
soft   supple
a mushy bog
a seaful of lipids drowning pores

fathers
sheath walls
rattle sabres

skeletons scorch leaves
flick
Kodak   Yashica   Konica

I   am   a   *coward*

where lips crease
like lines on a petal
trailing bloom

my tongue traces wildflowers

ripping, kneeling
wedging into the tips of
decayed scripture

scripture without revelation
for a choir without a cloistered roof
to contain the phrasing of mass

Ashhaduallah!

If one day
I throw in the towel

spasm crumbs   flour scents   mix persimmon

with

shroom   saffron   lychee

in a corrugated trip
strutted into the oven

without

a temperature gauge

timer knob

lay as detritus
on a kitchen table
as a forest triad

counting touches

what will our fathers say?

Anoint me in the stars
healing
curtains   doorways   gaps

Strange Fruit

'...And you could have it all / My empire of dirt /
I will let you down...' – Johnny Cash

///

pomegranates sleep unseen in aniline fuchsia, deseed
in Amorite and Eblaite clay-ducts under Mari so I draw

another fruit, vacant holes stare at a pedicel, this year
I draw less well, words brushstroke nipples to become

eyeballs, our window is porous for winter, Bonhoeffer
and cedars slate führers and verführers devising Lutheran

schism, kings, queens stare down earthly erections, pines
devise the book of bodies, coriander nights out of tune,

Charles Gounod blends operatic tradition to a language
of seamless sheaths - this picture, so wrong, so, so, wrong...

///

in the conservatory-converted-lounge walls page palanquined
princes, scenes from Fatehpur Sikri dome warring elephants

of the Mughal empire with space just for Alesha Popovich
so Hans Christian Anderson has to lie flat on the coffee-table

spine bent - I learn to accept my fate like Gene Krupa
dragging one stick across the snare head, keeping the beat

with the other stick - the matchstick girl in the open book
runs out of sticks, body-heat like I run out of the night...

///

I bury Ceasar, don't sing his praise beyond the favella
in lids unsealed for bacteria to facilitate decomposition,

jiggery reeds in lime to sweeten tongues, I paint turtles
dancing in Göbekli Tepe feet pointing down, a fresh

interpretation of the megaliths – one plays a dainty girl,
thorn-cut lips anticipating the southern tip of Kanyakumari

so the Cholas may follow sea-turtles, cross the Bay of Bengal
for cinnamon before compass, hoodwink puerperal clouds...

///

I eat lentils scooping the split seeds with my right hand
in runnels of cheek puffs and hollows letting out strange

sounds until early earth cools its rage in spume, I draw
shapes on the plate so Thamudic isn't classified as Safaitic

or Liḥyānite – I never learn to draw my own script on rocks
to differentiate records of goats from expressions of love

between boy-girl, boy-boy, girl-girl, shepherd and stone,
Muruwwah and sand, the honour code of Bedouins...

///

scribes wield crescent swords, reassure 1990, it snows
in Birmingham, my sister and I start a snowman but settle

for a Himalayan peak – we haven't seen the Kangchenjunga
or Shishapangma or Kedarnath or any peaks – it snows

just for a body to emerge in our lives with no head – our first
snow – we watch it melt sat by the coffee table where Edwin

is baptised on an open book, Coifi burns Celtic idols, like them
we barricade the whole afternoon, sheet walls for Penda...

///

this type of love, that between a brother and sister makes up
thirty-two years, we learn that citrus is not grape – citrine

flavedo is too pithy for distance – I return to amore-proper
bitten, crinkling and hardening a cusped arch for dahlias

sleepy in silence – this knowledge derived of inexperience
is not a priori, just inexperience, and my fingers reek bleach

after coital droplets in the hottest shower, scald dead skin,
cell a lifetime for the Northwind to run out of breath…

///

Southwind swallows the southern tip of Alkebulan, reaches
where the Frisians call other ~~Wales~~, Nanima smears

darkened soyabean oil in halua, reads from Thakurmar Jhuli,
a prince emerges metamorphosing the bedridden Gregor,

adults vex in a language I am yet to realise torrid grief,
and the cat who would press her forehead to mine sniffing

the right palm overlooking Furzton is not yet born so I watch
coots scour ripples, the fridge croons a strange fruit…

///

September weaves through a bosti, bodies coop in corrugated
shacks of tin and berra come rain in two-feet paths wall to wall,

Buriganga soars, Helen Schlegel hopelessly wanders the outskirts
for an untamed night, the last rain falls on the Hittite, Çatalhöyük

collapses into honeycomb caves without doors to keep out love
curling at the edge of lips at the first temple on earth, monoliths

seed in the central columns of grapes, bury the dead, carpels
grind a brief ten millennia, cuticles still tough to the human bite…

///

Eastwind reaches the castle of an irregular bear, the Westwind
drifts in tallow, I dream of Lake Bell smiling beast into bread,

but that's another story and the house becomes a girl washing
tallow off her prince, gerunds future fruits I just can't draw,

shapes fret the fretless, rababs lute from the hills of Pamir
to Bannau Brycheiniog, fairy wings swirl in the gentle heat

off a dwindling Windsor candle, the silver dulls for melodrama
I daren't bother *(for) beauty is nothing but the beginning*

*of terror, which we are just able to endure, every angel
terrifying,* Ailsa, Annabelle, the wych elm dust to dust…

/ / /

Muruwwah: spirituality invoking ancestor worship as practiced by pre-Islamic Arabs.

Northwind, Southwind, Eastwind & Westwind: characters in the Norwegian folk tale 'East
of the Sun and West of the Moon' included by Andrew Lang in "The Blue Fairy Book"
(1889)

Thakurmar Jhuli: a collection of Bengali fairy tales first published in 1907 that has remained
a firm favourite. Thakurma is grandmother in Bengali and jhuli is a traditional satchel. The
fairy tales bear some similarities in theme to folk tales from other parts of Asia and Europe.

'…beauty is nothing but the beginning of terror…': from Rainer Maria Rilke's 'Duino
Elegies'.

Turning Saints into the Sea

Stubborn pink scales a cliff-face becoming heather,
the sea crests hours instructing gulls to remember
nothing, footsteps totter in throat knots like a past

actuating days deigning the corners of each thirst,
meaningful as the sum of parts. Foxgloves stare
at distant elders wanting to grow tall, clumps of clay

grieve particle separation in tattered pots, spoon
voices pretending that words whispered here could
be heard in the furthest west of land where the fit

for communion jam a deceased willow, bodies
aureate song shaping ampersands. Dead-wood
feels no urge to chase the day after, a rotting boat

bobs twice a day for brief spells to sky-gaze inches
higher contemplating what penetrates its shell peeling
a shore to illicit touch, an axis fit for a crushed pigeon

who sacrificed himself in flight to remember a June
ending under a city ash for flesh to go their own way.

The Nearness of You

Scene: An early evening stroll through the third largest municipal burial ground in the UK, Cathays Cemetery, Cardiff.

Whisper beige, smear grey, earth into loam –
smother pebbles, stem green, here lies Joan;
daub pathways in ash, rowan, hazel, let jays fatten

on nuts, September grass to caress urns, mark time
in bracken for all three Edwards; breathe lichen,
splash an old hymn, hang it out to dry. In the fall

breeze by the nook for John and Margaret aslant
the stone, rise the Catholicus, chide the raindrops
falling on 'Morris 1923, Piermaster of Cardiff Docks',

watch time tumble, let rust tiptoe, waltz with holly,
pine and thorny berry, clutch bramble under a
Celtic cross, ivy Ebenezer, draping the pillar is

Christopher John, 'drowned at Porthcawl', aged
seventeen. Rest daisies on James, poke Cecilia,
watch a ladybird land on Rhoun, beloved wife to

Reverend William Green, perished at thirty-three;
let ghosts mutter in chapels, stack walls in finite
cracks under a railway bridge, scatter lost, trail

steps, here starts Roath. Let the robin flutter, pine
for a lost Scott, speckle gold to red, fly out to sit
upon the plaque – '...fell in love on this bench...';

stroll evenings in top hats, pristine white gowns,
Welsh cakes for high tea where Jack and Mary meet
John and Sallie; gates shut, sing dusk to elm-tops.

Drama/Trauma

Whether an event is deemed traumatic is defined by the 'subjective experience' of it rather than the event itself. – Trauma-informed care guidance

The briar perspires,
　　knuckles crack
the quiet, ankles bloat

beyond daylight
　　sputtering looks
fixed on April to ignite,

gods and grapes
　　brave nothing
for secrets exchanged

to hold the seasons
　　to account, warmer
each year, trains run late,

conical wheels course
　　the centre aligning
a differential

action self-centering
　　a reaction,
recompensing gravity

so when it rains it lashes,
　　you'd think
the cracks would

welcome moisture,
　　but the hardened
core repels warmth,

I am never
　　warm 'til
that fortnight's June,

the bud scale
     is a thick warm
sweater I wear all year

as a furry cover
     to flower
bigger, open earlier,

my leafers pop
     late in season,
thrips suckle, circle

obsessions, reveal
     vesicles in wings
wangling plots to tell

me I must aspire to be
     beautiful one
last time, smell vanilla.

The girl sat next
     shouts
on zoom something

about missing 'our
     mission',
I hear emission,

torsos sprawl
     on screen, slurp
tea, paint cups in

country rose, a tail
     perambulates
an edge, purrs, I notch

up 'adjust-appearance',
     wait my turn
for Holly to serve, throw

two bags into the white
        pot I sip, I want
to slurp the tectonic

uplift of the
        Himalaya eroding
sediments, flooding

what is left of the
        Brahmaputra,
but I compensate

for low light, I think last
        year's me
was wetter, lesser though

than the year gone
        or the ones before
until we are in a different

country and biscuit tins
        snap tight,
sickening sugar doughs

chomchom, butter
        beats in the back
of Baba's hand,

he is the driving seat,
        I am pinioned
to the back of a gurgling

Beetle, I ask Mamoni
        what is a gnome –
that which

we call a pose, she says,
        by any other same,
so one day I replace a d

with a t placating
    sacred tongues
vased in pre-industrial

levels of carbon dioxide,
    I sit down,
ask my friend

about the night
    u left
west Wales, two boys

clutching
    fingers
in postural control.

East of the Sun, West of the Moon

Yellow quivers inside the light bulb, nowhere
to go, a room is filled in the slow limbic mimicry

of curtains wind-washing faces, bodies coiling,
uncoiling, hands held, unheld, lips smeared

in yarrow, lips let gone, fur curled up in the
corner of the bed like a dusky marble cake –

years caught in sniffles I should put away for
good – acts in an over-stretched play, what

to write in, what to cross out, retire as ivy
gossip in ringlets. I am told that dried

neem leaves from back east keep out worms,
deter insects from chewing veins, shawls

come out creased only from the weight
of a dishevelled season shorn of hairballs.

I am scarred by feral summers – the wildest
feral never lets the eyelids kiss. I fear leaves

losing translucence to grow rings under my
eyes, make room for aging in guttural sighs

in dim turns around each room I enter, the
hours turning out all the lights and there is a

version of me stuck in another April of the
sharpest sting walking a full moon to find

laughter cackling in larches streaking sunlight,
goading ants sideways to climb up the limbs of

a last teen dawn. Tal-Y-Bont once advised each
new arrival to keep off the woods after dark so

hornbeams could creole nights into the embers
of a dewy auroral, buildings and trees could rise

to touch the skies, find new feet at their base to
stir into the morning tea. Old Ken I knew, once

said that *youth is wasted on the young*. I want to
penance all my days combined, sniff aster to the

chime of ropey leashes clattering flagpoles, let a
red dragon hovel green and white, inherit the wind.

Chocolate

Combat18: definition: a neo-Nazi terror organization was founded in 1992, suspected of perpetrating vicious attacks on people of colour, with reported deaths across UK, Germany and Canada, although most attacks may have gone unreported.

Once / the one to the left snapped / submerged in Cadbury's Fruit and Nut / fresh from the fridge / every so often / they have to be glued back /

Mr Kochak / the dentist says / "There's nothing to hold them in for good" / slotting them back into the metal he had drilled /

I remember his anaesthetic needle / piercing the pink of the gum / a dagger easing itself back into its own sheath / the body was ready this time / felt no pain /

I have taught myself to bite with the incisors / avoid the molars / if I had balls / I'd glue them back in the bathroom mirror / each time they snap / if I had tears / I'd mourn / save myself from the dentist's chair /

Pristine white / white as frost / on a punt / gliding down the river / letting the sun / toast them into me / varnish-tarnish / their darkest sheen / still white / never in fear /

Down by the river nothing cries / hemlock / Himalayan raspberry / huddle my spot / wild petunia spread wings / unburden / become butterflies / trample ripples on Ely /

The river is a green god / sometimes brown / the fish / the mallards / and I / crouch / all summer / all winter / suckle particles of air / floating above / dangle chocolate feet / in proskynesis/ watch white tan / water becoming wine /

Her white / cupping / my / hand / dragonflies on tips of ripples / a precarious balancing act / rise and fall / how can the minutes be stitched back / to feed the skin / tell a tale / her two-toned hair / lips awaiting a bite / I am so hungry to bite /

Tell her / why I cycle miles / sleep with lights on / what happens in darkened alleys when the gods aren't watching /

I free my hands off her / off all / disappear / into the woods / to distant
rivers / Padma-Meghna-Jamuna / watch ants carry their own to a feast /
a funeral pyre /

Girls and boys walk fingers clasped / past crepuscule / a sun and a moon
leer above the rooftops / bodies dressed for the night / through the
narrowest stretch / steaming / and I now take the main road each time /
to reach Spar /

Ribs healed / retina reattached / I sit by the river / watch bodies toast /
let go of touch /

Bodies winter scrubbed / toothpaste white / run through the city / cross
continents / suburbs / Northcote Lane / all hours / their bite into frozen
'Fruit and Nut' / no knife glinting / a body bouncing back and forth
against a garage door / rope-a-dope / roll on asphalt / the night stills /

Missa Solemnis

Scene: A plaque for Dr Christopher Hoddell, 1957-94,
on a Llandaff Cathedral cemetery bench.

Rust mildew
    shapes in rain
    two feet shy, leaves

glyph runes
    on oily ravines
    wet skin

macerate
    stories gone
    fables to tell

a nook of leaves.
    Tonight, cyclops
    may gobble satyrs

the dark is finding shape
    wagtails may rouge cheeks
    line boundaries

define moments, let the gone
    gawk at faces
    edging a sinking sun.

In a step (or two)
    the last light arcs in
    vespers curling

stone cracks, the dark
    clamps ancient rock, moss
    hems the fog

in the field behind
    probing, is it time
    to head back

or *a time to start?*

The caterpillar cleans
    itself each summer
    at the end of each

unpredictable stint of
    rain, a stout beak
    yellows the skin

in the fading light, is it
    a shag or a cormorant
    tickling Taff?

How to tell
    the difference, what
    defray, promises

made to lips
    sat on a bench, backs
    pressed in anticipation

pressing a rectangle
    a small golden plaque
    Kyrie, Credo, Agnus Dei.

Amygdala

Moral Liberty is the power of following, in all circumstances, our sense of right and wrong; or of acting in conformity to our reflecting and moral principles, without being controlled by any contrary principles. – 'A Review of the Principal Questions in Morals', 1758, Richard Price. Price is widely acknowledged to be the greatest philosopher and political thinker born in Wales.

All my Marches accumulate rubble, the rain struggles
       in its bid to silence a structure under the temporal lobe,

an almond shapes beneath the uncus, diverse, complex
       comprising 13 nuclei to decode a room with no door.

I wore Yves Klein in a Paris studio for my birthday,
       a new blue, darker than Bengal 1859, the indigo skin

of Kader Molla drained of its worthlessness: to be
       worthless is not being entirely devoid of worth,

but to be worth less than what is being compared to.
       My heart keels in need, a house weans itself off guilt

pretending it is the waun, the Biafra embroider pine
       for the land swallowed, limpets periwinkle erosion,

venerate wells, make up tales of saints snorkelling
       the Atlantic as black grouse. I have held on to a post-it

note once sticky, ~~pretty~~, I save it for a day that never
       comes to write my manifesto on the right of men

to lie on broken futons. The noxious sprouts ladders
       for a fallen sapling in the garden where flowers have

forgotten the basics of shredding an unwritten
       song in mini-bar ink for a 4th ~~of~~ July. I syncopate

Charles Lloyd scraping cantos through the shared
       earphone and America is born so Terrance Hayes

can *carry a flag bearing a different nation on each*
          side. In the city of Jahangir, four hundred years

in bodies lean out, face the subtropical afternoon
          flame, a lone peanut seller sinks an orange sun

above Hatkhola on his top of the voice *rakben*
          badam. I unravel in the folds of a sari, a horse

on a boat pops out the same size inside a glass jar
          seen at four, compiles the red list of birds I shall

never see again, my perished father spinning muslin
          mutters *what price is independence* when the tokai

foliates lyres in original sin, digs for congealed
          bhat in the municipal waste, how Paul Simon

carries real estate America for Cathy in his pocket
          on a bus ticket to Saginaw. Lambs graze a world

I once liked. I've given up on virtue or the unitary
          nature of god as the universal creator of dynamics

phrasing a yelp through streets impersonating
          the bloated demolition of an illicit underpass.

Kader Molla: one of the leaders of the 1859 Nil Bidroho (Indigo Revolt) in Bengal when rice farmers refused to cultivate indigo instead of food crops, and defied the colonial East India Company rule.

Rakben Badam: translated from Bengali, 'Would you like to buy peanuts?'

Tokai: an impoverished young child looking for food or potentially sellable items in open municipal bins in Bangladesh. The root of the noun refers to 'a gatherer' in Bengali.

Bhat: rice

57

Sanctuary

40 something Abu Bakr (not his real name), a speaker of many North African tongues, flees persecution and finds himself in South Wales. His body is scarred from the ravages of a journey acquainted with nights under the stars. On his first day, he wanders through the historic arcades of Cardiff city centre, gets lost and finds himself by the fowl filled Feeder Canal towards Cardiff Bay. How can the ducks be so trusting? He secures work as a food delivery rider, carrying flavours of the world to Cardiff homes.

I pretend I have arrived, made it, that I am capable of shifting
form, colour, the shape of my tongue to make up fresh sounds.

Some days I wander through the arcades enset to mint, basil
to pistachio, bean too keen, I flit through pantones, become

an emerald sage, seaweed for a vegan crocodile, a pear for a
willing juniper, gin to pearl. Other days I am a scented geranium

with crinkly golden-edged leaves. In the afternoons I am galangal
– aurvedic ginger, and when it rains, I hold up my shirt to gather

the drizzle, watch it ooze lemon verbena. I marvel at my prowess
to assemble a flock of fowl (maybe, just one), I imitate, wear

the brightest green, a shade to fit in with the mallard eating
off my palm, I want it to drip gratitude, smear my lifeline

in saliva in spite of the duck tongue incapable of dripping
endearments, but I am forgiving, I can tolerate the avian

salivary glands huddling along the hard palate of the bill letting
the feed coat, ease the swallow. I don't limit my need to be

cleansed in this pretence – he licks my palm with an imagined
tongue, barges the ankle with the starboard of his plume, a nudge

to remind my green is put on. What if I am merely a vessel
between the minaret and the genuflect, a device in a masterplan

to feed creatures great and small? What if the whole city was
a vessel? A sanctuary for hollyhocks aiming too high, hiraeth

sung in each doorway for shores left behind, cells of moss
bursting unasked to secrete droplets to quench each thirst

until the last brown blackbird silences for the night after all the
bombs have been dropped, boats huddling muffles have set sail

across channels, each streetlamp filled with estuarinedfrond
pouncing in tongues to shape words never heard in this land?

Snapdragons Need the Bulk of Bumblebees to Force Open the Flower

Cicadas become conspiratorial spiders,
    evolve in extraction vaults, investigate ways
        of savouring the inedible, prod a garden oak
           to defy its century ~~landlady wanted it cut~~.

Furzton seethes in its yearning for quiet,
    the lake bloats to ford hard rain, tributaries drown
        stepping stones, the age irons out of its flakes,
           bones calcify, hide. The Watling scours footsteps

in earthen mounds chatting up euphorbia,
    automatons in antennae commune with distant
        isles, grind to a halt at first sight of moveable flesh,
           city boulevards coddle roundabouts

each identical, arachnids tender resignation,
    whizz undone, clouds dome dandelions, boreen fog
        lisp the veiled Iceni, vapour and ghosts scatter
           too soon. The moon burrs half-burnt a flatbread,

shines just for the gods, constructs hollows,
    mopes the songbird flown to warm pots
        of honey spreading sunsets to release
           fireflies dreaming ceilings in dahlias,

bullfinches plant holly to mark entrances,
    become addicted to seeds, scribe each day
        for a hungry interior stacked in light. I curl
           up in a bed made of sails, coots chatter

the night, slugs recluse millimetre at a time,
    willow barges into poplar, hawthorn
        into blackthorn, moorhens eyeing lapwings
           imitate calls, waver flight, become plovers.

All day I pine wisteria, absolve
    the skin's need to purple in transit,
        crows building nests from scratch fill
            my mouth with leftovers past the discarnate

brood of legs atoning a duvet raiding
    nothing, cobwebs descend, shape pillows,
        leave room, fracture a lakebed in seaglass,
            shards twist in winding chimneys, whisper Boudica.

Anda

'Such grief does not desire consolation. It feeds on the
sense of its hopelessness. Lamentations spring only from
the constant craving to re-open the wound.'
– "Brothers Karamazov", Fyodor Dostoevsky

Bolt all doors, latch windows, let steam
fester. Daal lingers long past the plates

scraped. The other night I cracked halua:
grate your carrots thin, shear in index-skin,

watch a sunset grind yellow into orange,
bleed. Smoke gathers a room away burning

logos, clarifying butter – churn baby churn,
ghee another year, a glass tomb to sensate

a crane's yearning for coronal fire. Why,
to preserve what? Rosewater clears

the palette, what rises falls, evenings circle,
groan, cling to Cathays, woodpigeons

articulate their thirst for gravel. Winter
broke me like a speckled thrush on its

tangled pine for almanacs. I predict drizzle
startling the corners of windowsill moss,

starlight and moonlight and amorous
melodies thickening bounteous spores

to reassert green. This morning, my
sister lit her Belling, I had not smelt

sugar suppurating anda in three
decades inside a house, her home:

Scrat and Thumper sneak in under
the fence yet to gauge what business

the wagtail has with perished leaves,
I dream all day of being an ill-fitting

cardigan, slouch forget-me-nots among
sleet. Inward fog flutters in the distance

confusing nomenclature, remains
itself. The self. I am west. My abode

is a Welsh fridge. The top-shelf
caresses the frosted element slowing

death, halting birth, the last little
tupperware my mother filled two

years before she dies and I save
the last dollop, mould-clad like her

disintegrating body, soft tissue aching
communion, skeletal, drifting prayer.

Anda: the word for egg in Bengali, which shares its shape with the number zero or 'shunno',
a word used as a literary term referring to nothingness, absence or vacancy, and therefore in
common use, 'anda' means nothing or nothingness.

The Substrate of a Rose

At the water's edge wild grass
foliate rustle, the quarter moon

bugles a wisp of lit, clouds
star in their own tattering,

emerald ducks stab bills, paddle,
manoeuvre shapes past dusk,

yearn for lips. January is an
orphaned liturgy, the oleander

months off pink, a trailing censer
salt-and-pepper mumble under

the chin, scratch the cold injustice
of now, the unknown stein, what

mead or manoeuvre shall spring
come in when the sorrel discover

benches cleared of moss? An austere
calyx dressed as grandfather time

once walked Hall Green, his
rosewood caning each asphalt

inch, the sepal of each flower
disturbed in the thud of wanting

answers to lost hearing, sight
wavering towards the unheard

green rose drifting to the edge
of a pious evening. What piety

made me run at sixteen my
fastest, eyes wanting to be

a song, laminae of the gales
digging elk-bones? Now the aim

is to understand mortar, all its
beguiling viscosity, why the Tang

smothered rice flour into theirs,
how Anatolian mosques withstood

comets and the underearth, rise
as minarets feigning death. And,

how shall I expiate my sins past
the fiqh of want, susurrate

an old world tome, make out
the genus of flies peppering

the green rose on the banks
of Acheron? I am still moved

by song. Why? The honeydew
untasted rubs a whiskered chin

of primrose, benediction, the birth
of hope and despair, I baptise you

with air. Thou shalt fall in love with
the dryad, plant acorns, fixity is daal.

Fiqh: an Arabic word meaning 'full understanding', the word is also used to refer to
Islamic jurisprudence.

Ramadan

The hours play out each shadow: bluebells,
wild garlic, the flowering quince spread

each inch of the morning, I measure their
three sixty turns elongating, shortening,

drowning the first hint of bumblebees. The
clock wasps, amoral lashes keep tab on

the lengthening minutes of the sun, I
serenade each fly landing on thighs wanting

to be exposed, I want to subjugate restless
souls by lying still, splash savage wings in

lachrimae murmuring non-violence
incanting the whole lunar month – this

whole April, my merciful axe is a blade
sheathed in bacchanal, daddy-long-legs

still forming, fit snug inside my half-glass
lent out to the wind. At the vertex of sun

I dream up a tramontane, a gust to figwort
my glands, quench each parch. The day

done, at sunset I am mad, certified, I've
re-lived all the berries crushed, and in

Kincraig St the calla lily in the garden front
looking up to the last of the crimson, its

spadix thrusting a yellow pine for the sky
drifting from the milky spathe wanting to

hold on, I walk past unacknowledged – I'm
on a mission to calm the guttural Bay of

Bengal. The first droplet is a lightning rod
flute to temper each sand-grain fit for a

palm to dip, imprint a dusky maghrib
azan – the day then begins all over again.

Aurora Out of Time

Summer communes with the pits blackening sleeves.
An itch drapes backs of chairs, a sun lit for squirrels
in shallows and cantons snide at dragonflies, moths
colour in their own hindwings, mark forewings,

moths who know their former selves – caterpillars
in black and golden stripes. Sparrows flap their wings
to maximise thrust, preserve energy, move air beyond
the twittering jinns in forms that only jinns are at will

to assume. Who governs their speculation, the mischief,
syllables crushing dusk for twilight sin? Taps drip at ten
to scour ladles, pots darken, grime hardens for hands
to scrub, a fly torments the skylight, rows with patterns

on a bowl, thuds the sink, licks glutes off a last supper,
disappear. Ankles take knee striped for Fajar: ablution
is to ignore the pain of kneecaps stinging prayer-mats,
father, cat and the holy mist vase rojonigondha for none.

Jinn: according to the Quran, jinns are created by Allah like humans, but they are made of light, often whimsical, and can assume animate or inanimate forms to trick or aid humans.

Rojonigondha: a resplendent summer night's flower common in Bangladesh known as tuberose in English, often referred to as the 'queen of the night'.

What Are You Doing
The Rest Of Your Life

We must be willing to let go of the life we have planned,
so as to have the life that is waiting for us. – E M Forster

Lake-breeze pokes sunlit errors. Bees clump
repeating the same note in rose-pink
spiraea, leaves

ovate a winding path unworthy of the body, ·
Furzton flats and sharps inside
a coated

wooden hammer to dismantle the gone.
The sun is too bright. I can't
differentiate between

the weight of sin in blossom and guava jam
two decades old sticking to the base
of a jar past its maker,

this empire stretches amra, gaab, daab, sours
the formation of phlox, footsteps
thrum unknown keys,

open no doors, chainsaws cut distant vines
on roads before the age
of cycle-paths,

mechanised mowers grit teeth for mornings
to sleep still at half past ten,
green malingers

in the linden and the lime, Dravidic tongues
inflect Kerala, shatter invisible
coconuts into tales

circulating Lidl and the Woodville: tales
of how this skin is blotchy,
has taken on memory,

wrists wrinkled, corners of nails gawking
ponytails in flicks and frets.
Gravel loops

in Egyptian terry shy of the sea sleeping
in heraldic strokes two miles
off, tender kahins

summon tufts of light too far to inherit,
the wind chimes secrets in reeds
sifting green

no right to be this soft with no past, a canal
winds to distemper alders,
clouds scatter

devious pores to deflower the distance between
two points on a map a month
short of 28 years

straight as the heron's dart, duckweed docks
Novello and Dahl in loins let lost,
at Cadwaladers'

almonds deconstruct ridges of cream for ice
to crackle, the ceiling moves
front to back,

skin mulls memory in foam for dawns to reconcile
form on mattress. Flesh immures ketones
for the fridge-grown

fungus to puff air so lowly junipers yet to bear
the weight of sin may breathe
fresh, quake

aspens in the lightest breeze in tombed esplanades
of the darkest limbs, ash sleeves
for the story ended.

Amra, gaab, daab: seasonal fruits common in Bangladesh and in East Bengal, India.

Acknowledgements

My thanks to the editors where the following poems had first appeared in:

Yashica 635 and Internal Reliquary in *Anthropocene*, Butter, Chocolate and Muktijoddha in *Poetry Wales*, Seamstress in *South Bank Poetry*, Teach Jackdaws Avionics in *Propel*, Bread of Heaven in *Love the Words, International Dylan Thomas Day Prize Anthology*, A Morning Walk in *Honest Ulsterman*, The Free State of Roath in *Interpreter's House*, Animal Wall in *Maps & Rooms, Writings from Wales* anthology published by Lucent Dreaming, Stars siphon narcissus so in *Atrium*, A Pond for All Eels, Turning Saints into the Sea and Missa Solemnis in *The Lonely Crowd*, East of the Sun, West of the Moon and Ramadan in *Bad Lilies*, Ramadan also in *The Aesthetica Creative Writing Award Anthology 2023*, Amygdala in *Free Verse, Poems for Richard Price*, published by Seren Books, Sanctuary in *Planet – The Welsh Internationalist,* Anda and What Are You Doing the Rest of Your Life in *Acropolis Journal*. The Substrate of a Rose was commissioned by the *Abridged* magazine as a response to the Nina Simone song 'Sinnerman'.

I had spent much time studying contemporary poetry at the National Poetry Library in London and utilising the poetry collection at the Cardiff Central Library. My thanks to the librarians associated with these institutions.

The following editors specifically encouraged me at very crucial stages of my development as a poet: Emily Trahair, Jeremy Noel-Tod, Kathryn Gray, Andrew Nelson, Aaron Kent, Jonathan Edwards and Zoë Brigley.

I'd also like to thank the following for their encouragement, kindness and for being inspirational – Jon Gower, Hanan Issa, Nasia Sarwar-Skuse, Hammad Rind, Alun Gibbard, Natalie Ann Holborow, Eric Ngalle Charles, John McCullough, and lastly, my sister Karishma Rabbi and my late mother, Professor Khadija Rahman.

Thanks to Gillian Clarke who had personally selected me to be part of her week-long poetry masterclass as part of the 30th birthday celebration of the Tŷ Newydd writing school, Writerz and Scribez for selecting me for a six week community poetry masterclass with Caleb Femi, Literature Wales for part funding the 'Climate Change Writing retreat' at the Black Mountain College with course leaders Tom Bullough and Jay Griffiths, and also for selecting me to be part of the 2023 Hay Festival 'Writers at Work' development programme administered by Tiffany Murray. Literature Wales as an organisation have supported me from the very start. Without being selected for the Representing Wales 2021 writer development programme and the subsequent mentorship opportunity with Zoë Brigley, the road to this very first collection would have been significantly longer and harder. My special thanks to Amy Wack, the former Seren poetry editor for seeing something in me back in 2019 and her continued encouragement, and to Rhian Edwards and Zoë Brigley, the present editors, and everyone at Seren Books for their immense kindness.

Special thanks to my dear friend and confidant Lottie Williams for reading the first completed drafts of most of these poems, suggesting that some of our mundane Instagram conversations could become poems, and for believing in me.

Finally, Zoë Brigley has been an immense rock as my mentor and editor. The journey to this collection and the many development opportunities she has pushed me towards would not have happened without her unflinching support. I remain eternally grateful.

All that jazz:

Music, musicians and composers have a strong presence as reference, inspiration or part of a quirky compositional process in this collection. The genres range from jazz to classical as well as popular music by Simon and Garfunkel, Lennon and McCartney and others. Jazz, however, dominates the musical references and inspirations.

However, the specific themes of individual poems had not allowed for mentions of the musical references in epigraphs or endnotes.

It is the nature of jazz that the music and lyrics had often been written at different times. At times, popular songs, particularly from Broadway shows had inspired musicians to transcribe or syncopate the music to virtuosic heights. Where jazz finds itself in specific poems, the inspiration and influence may have come from the music, the lyrics or a combination where the vocal version of a song exists, as well as specific versions recorded or performed by specific musicians. The following denote some of the major musical influences behind this collection: 'East of the Sun (and West of the Moon)' written by Brooks Bowman lends itself as the title of eponymous poem as well as the collection, with the version recorded by the singer and pianists Diana Krall being of principal influence.
Saxophonist John Coltrane's version of 'My Favorite Things', originally from the Rodgers and Hammerstein musical 'The Sound of Music', had part inspired the poem 'Animal Wall'. Pianist Brad Mehldau's version of Paul McCartney's 'Blackbird', which had minor lyrical contribution from John Lenon, had inspired a number of poems, including 'The Nearness of You'.

The song 'What Are You Doing The Rest Of Your Life', written and orchestrated by Alan Bergman, Marilyn Bergman and Michel Legrand, lends itself as the title of the final poem in this collection. It also part inspired 'I Want to See Your Face in Every Kind of Light', 'The Free State of Roath' and 'Animal Wall'. Versions of the song to have been of particular influence have been recorded or performed by pianist Bill Evans and singers Frank Sinatra and Annabelle Johnson.

'Blame It On My Youth', written and orchestrated by Oscar Levant and Edward Heyman part inspired 'The Free State of Roath', in particular, recordings by singer and trumpeter Chet Baker, pianists Keith Jarrett and Brad Mehldau, and singer Nat King Cole and Rita Payes.

'The Nearness of You', written and orchestrated by Ned Washington and Hoagy Carmichael inspired the eponymous poem. The significant versions were by singer Norah Jones, Nat King Cole, Ella Fitzgerald and Louis Armstrong, pianists Bill Evans and Brad Mehldau, saxophonist Joshua Redman and bassist Charlie Haden.

'Spring Is Here' written and orchestrated by Hans Spialek and Richard Rodgers had part inspired 'Ramadan', 'Teach Jackdaws Avionics', 'What Are You Doing The Rest Of Your Life' and 'Internal Reliquary'. The version of the song to have been of specific influence was recorded by double bassist Charlie Haden and pianist Kenny Barron for the album 'Night and the City'.

'Willow Weep for Me' composed by Ann Ronell and the specific versions sung by Billie Holiday and Nina Simone had influenced the poems 'Stars siphon narcissus so' and 'Anda'. Will Holt and Les Baxter composed an early version of the song 'Sinnerman', and singer and pianist Nina Simone rearranged the most famous version of the song. Editor Susannah Galbraith from the 'Abridged' magazine had commissioned the poem 'The Substrate of a Rose' as a response to 'Sinnerman'.

The song 'Strange Fruit' written by Abel Meeropol and recorded by Billie Holiday as a musical protest to highlight the lynching of black Americans inspired elements of the poem bearing the song title.

One of the most popular jazz standards 'Autumn Leaves' was originally composed by Joseph Koshma as a French song 'Les Feuilles mortes', and the song part inspired the poems 'Teach Jackdaws Avionics', 'Trap Arachnids for Rainy Days' and 'Turning Saints into the Sea' through the specific versions recorded by Chet Baker, singer and trumpeter, and Miles Davis.

'America', a song written by Paul Simon sung by Art Garfunkel and Paul Simon had distinctly influenced the poem 'Amygdala'.

The self-harm and addiction themed song 'Hurt' was written by Trent Reznor and originally recorded by the American band Nine Inch Nails. The harrowing version later recorded by Johnny Cash part inspired the poems 'Strange Fruit' and 'Permission'.